The Bunny Poems

Also by David Caddy

Poetry
The Balance (1981)
Anger (1982)
The Beating on the Door (1987)
Honesty (1990)
Continuity (1995)
Desire (1997)
The Willy Poems (2004)
Man in Black (2007)

Criticism
So Here We Are (2011)

Literature
London: City of Words (with Westrow Cooper, 2006)

The Bunny Poems

DAVID CADDY

Shearsman Books

First published in the United Kingdom in 2011 by
Shearsman Books
50 Westons Hill Drive
Emersons Green
Bristol
BS16 7DF

http://www.shearsman.com/

ISBN 978-1-84861-195-5

Acknowledgements
Thank you to the editors of *Denver Syntax Quarterly, Fire, Gists & Piths,
Hanging Johnny, Nth Position, Peony Moon, Pirene's Fountain,
Ragged Edge, Rewords, Shadow Train* and *Veer About*
where some of these poems were originally published.

I would like to thank Sarah Hopkins for her close reading of the
manuscript and Louise Anne Buchler for her encouragement.

Contents

The Bunny Poems

For Louise Anne Buchler

I

Natural Facts

1

Gypsy kids skin stags leaving guts
outside Frampton House for all to see.
Poaching pools clutch knives
slit throats make a heap of heads,
telling Taylor he can stuff his shoot.
Animal rescue workers fight
like ferrets in a bag,
occupying a quaint urban quarter.

When a man knew horseshit from sprays
could count lapwings, was paid in pence.
When a man knew bend from hack,
near from far, grist from grizzle,
it was all subterranean, somehow
so hidden and unsaid like a kettle
with a silent whistle. A concentration,
a deepening of the gaze.

2

At home we came to speech late
sometimes not at all.
Fear of sky, those higher,
bound us to village, the call.
Following trails across Three Corners
a stillness clings to boundary.
How the template can break,
be lived as something else.

We ate incessantly, like broilers,
storing for those times that might come
that might steal us from mother.

We ate in silence. Instead of emotion,
pigs and dogs one knew and fed.
In the face of thought, undug plots,
grass to be cut, the lure of light.
An absence of fruit, reading matter.

Yes

Mother turned the mangle's stiff handle,
wringing out the last drops into a bowl,
her damp hands as white as cat gut.

Leaving the door open to let the wood smoke out,
I caught the cold and blackbird song
that spoke with clouds and light.

Stripped to the bone, gaps, white stones,
to pore and drift within and without,
I found space and emptiness to lift.

In the open field that was our house
irresistible lives crossed our paths, curled
round posts lying deep, leaving us replete.

Blurred

No explanation is offered
when the old barn burns down.
No one wants to follow
into the three mile wood.
In 1961 it is enough
to believe in electricity.

A dark awareness rooted
in broken branches, absence of song,
strangling webs, a healing stag's foot,
the remains of a bonfire,
what could be moving, or forced to,
catches an eye, jolts.

Pausing, mid-stride, to look left,
adjust the step and suspend
the slap of recognition.
Drips, echoes. Stoat ripped
flesh. Muffled clips, snaps.
Something nervous, blurred, calls out.

Sturminster Market

Fiercely honed faces
framed in starch white coifs,
uniform black dresses to mid-calf
are absent.

Men standing around the corner
intent on cups of tea,
the cool chatter behind bar and urn,
occasionally lean away.

A rutted dirt track
rows of cars, carts
clusters of men, boys
in stratified groupings.

Creased jacket, hat in hand,
awkwardly staunch and stern,
he squints at the hated men
ringed and bidding.

He stands and waits.
Calves squeal. His feet are cold.
Ham stone horses hurl defiance,
an ossified anguish.

After-birth

Back in the days of centre partings,
when gentlemen doffed their hats to strangers
and old people were those that walked
into the river or hid under a bridge,
I had a dog called Sue.

The wind told her a fantastic story.
I caught the periphery of her vision.
We jumped the wire fence that subsided
in our making and lifted our legs
to meet whatever lay ahead.

She burned for days. Implied
that I should prod the door, walk out
with a stick. She slept in the tool shed,
with the jackdaw, by the paraffin heater,
and never came on heat. I minced her tripe.

Someone was lost, trying to find a way.
We walked a steady line along the
grind, ears pricked, negotiating real
and perceived obstacles with trust and luck,
waiting for the next call or crack.

I could read, hear the breeze listening in,
following a trail that began to stare back
in more than distance. My foreboding
appeared in a rush from the legs of a woman
and Sue growled long and hard at our find.

Harry in His Last Year of Employment

He brought his milk round with him, clicking
in his mouth, when we entered the hot room.
Harry in his last year of employment and I
in my first. Two greenhorns hugging baskets
of yellow curd towards an electric hopper.
Crumbs, an acrid smell, filling our open shirts.

Harry sifts bird calls in his frequent blows.
His wholeness drifting in bits of past lives.
Stone picker. Bird scarer. Stone-breaker,
hauler. Road builder in the Twenties and Thirties.
Turns on the boundary of speech, takes
seconds to reply to a question or an order.

Leaning over hot vats to cut and turn,
forcing sword like knives inwards two-handed
as if punting, exhaling every second, third stroke.
Two men attempting to carefully empty top hats,
trimming their edges, restoring body, shape,
relentlessly told to empty yet more vats.

Harry rubs both nostrils with his forefingers
as if shaving off some unwanted flakes.
Vision ceases as the hopper clogs. Wedges
removed. Hands opened to release distant
dreams. Recaptured as the connection sparks.
Whiff of rennet, old man, wet coat.

Harry spits. The pour of his head wringing out
inner strength. Veins in full display. Effort
effervescent. Between bursts, he inspects callouses.
He insists on filling the muslin covered moulds

refusing impulses to slow down, their sheer volume
seemingly a challenge to his name's aura.

He thrusts his shovel to the trolley bottom
and in measured experience presses his weight
sideways on, whilst I with nimbler hands
weigh, fold muslin, remove pins, apply the pump
re-weigh and place on the press room belt.
We become a team. Old-timer. A-level student.

By hose down he's nearly spent. Handkerchief knotted.
I offer to take the shovel. Am met with an iron
no and cannot grasp. I sulk. We do not speak.
Other workers avoided the shovel, sniggered.
Later I saw marks on the scales, his fear, and
Harry lost two fingers in the hopper, and left.

No Burning Cottages

Eight became six, six became four,
some men could not hack it anymore,

left early, took to dog racing, pigeons,
making bird tables, rearing pheasants,

cropped up in garages under apprentices,
in cheese factories, garden centres.

A gradual absence, with their world
of signs and recognition dispersed

like husks. No great noise. No burning
cottages. Consent on the brink of sense.

Each year less rows of runner beans,
washing. Wildflowers altering the balance

of things, shifting feet, stones.
Some turning authority, duration

on its head, placing this against that,
and staying put, not listening

to the spaces between worlds.
Susceptibility taking them like magic.

Alfie Does Not Speak Much Now

Dorset tenor does not speak much. Harsh mum.
Acquiescent dad. Storm forms and lasts.
Gradual to sudden invasion of dying people,
houses priced out of local reach, cows in fields.

Was lean to shed, doing time, mind slant
numinous creature to the locked lollard,
keeper of birds, hens and beans, skull herd,
hot room surgeon to flinch and buckle.

Was gaunt in the sun and rented room, crew
cut, get it right cheese maker, not so cheeky,
sing a long, what's that in the magician's hat,
that T. Cooper moment, mild analgesic, aspirin.

Alfie spits tobacco, his first and index fingers
tightly holding a roll-up, his right arm arcing
outwards and down. His stare fixed, seemingly
intent upon some distant object. Quiet bull.

Now owl, lady's bedding, dace out of school,
ace in the hole in an underworld of muteness,
nod and nudge, flutterer of bets, plough of silence,
confederacy of dunces, apocrypha and apocryphal.

From the Farm

Head bowed, walking up and down
the street, in pursuit of his past,
trembling at the prospect of vocation.

He carries an animal's face on him.
Light emanates from its enormous
eyes and nose. He cannot let go.

He is from the farm and the farm
has not let him go. Wrapped within,
he sneezes, missing more than woman.

As a boy he strode down the hill
to sing in church with the village.
Those people have been and gone.

He lifts his shoulders, accepting
the weight of absences, and clings
to the next moment of stillness.

The Orchard and Herb Garden

What could be moving, or forced to,
catches an eye, the slap of recognition.

Whiff of sawdust. Darkness closing in.
White thistles stiffly upright eavesdropping.

Night air, at freezing, no support
coming on, only shots of malt.

I cannot speak. There should be something
to keep this hurt from filling my gut.

A snap. To savour and protect
the peculiar from the bland. To taste.

Bite at odds with lustre. Eyes and ears,
stretch to that moment of release.

My thoughts, as flat as the hanging horseshoe,
on an anvil of significance and cost.

Young Paul Hart

Full of passion Mississippi Paul Hart
Shunter Smith And His Boogie Train
brashly erects his first art poster in Stur
and the locals are ecstatic at the Biba hint,
there is a clap of praise and we are
moved to believe in the divine again.

At the Fiddleford, cold on the table waiting, two pints of 6X.
A ritual, man to man, glass by glass, until chucking out.
LA Woman in the air. Paul's declarative. Art portfolio.
MG parked askew. He's got two women, the fuzz on his trail.
He's a Friend of the Devil. He's my friend. He's maybe your
friend too. He knows Matisse, chords, runs thirty miles daily,
will help you if you ask. His smile does not lie. We lie under
its gravitas, alive in the valley and try to be the best that we can
and not some shady agent who hides words under the spit of
their tongue.

He slumps down, covering the table with papers, and says
without vision, we only see parts, we are pistils and stamens.

Serena

Before the by-pass and Bristol raiders,
I used to visit the Italian in West Street
with its signed pictures of starlets,
octogenarian, dog and Serena,
immaculate in tight skirt, mobile, artificial
leather, barely disguised fatigue.

The owner would sometimes appear
with fat cigar, smile and shrug.
I recalled my old economics teachers
saying that monetarists were a mad
fringe group that would never come to power.

When the Italian closed we moved
our allegiance to Sarah's in East Street,
and Serena, in new pinstripe, answered
her last call and never came back.

From Small Things

She stands in Salisbury Street calculating
uncollected income against council tax,

catches the flight of a single bullfinch
that lands on a gutter to look and listen.

Her boyfriend keeps owls and makes his own
furniture. He works as a night watchman

seven days on and seven days off. He likes
sitting beneath a tree, identifying sounds,

scouring skips; collects farm memorabilia.
She smiles, notes gaps, recalls The Good Life

where she would barter with Richard and talk
to Tom, the playwright, about politics,

catches a stranger's bright scarf,
her mind moving further from small things.

Rapacious

Please let me feed the dog

and catch my breath

from this halo-light,

the rampant swarm in concatenation

fiery of root and thigh

voracious

keep of feta,

active curiosity, contagion.

A bowl of sweetness

ripens, ravening

upended

lusty to lip

smocks of wondrous heat

individually, collectively

resuscitate on top

cupped.

Hilfield Friary

The heart's alive to what's invisible
in the opulence of pistil and stamen.
There's a thrusting between spaces,
a body drained and laden coming to rest.

Despite a lifted headache I cannot
submit to more than a brief uphill
walk and infinite sleep. Entered
being the key word rather than penetrated.

Here the Brothers beguile in simplicity
mark time with prayer, tasks and tea,
clock individual nuances that rise
penny-like out of succulent visitation.

Sharp May wind carries gunshot,
rattling trains and carts far away.
Only the gunshot insists on this rote
of battle between self and identity.

Old drains and gullies filter downstream,
with cargo both toxic and benign,
reek of absence, by the black Christ,
and echo contemplation once more.

Birch

I miss the touch and white of your thought
subtle and silver as the autumn air
moving in delicate waves.

Each season more margins melt.
Stillness disappears against
dogma's sway.

Sane and sequent creatures stumble
in the breath of your quiet absence.

II

Bunny's Landscape
after Michelle Noteboom

1

Drift in the counter direction and it feels like hail
sweeping over the hills and pounding on your door

when you wastrel, you cannot look down shafts of
wormholes and don't see the marauding earwigs

centipedes and dung beetles congregating by your step
and foot stool. Look at those events, births and deaths,

luncheons, not as inconsequential to your employment,
to your devotion to history, to three dimensional

coordinates, line and volume, the fallacies of
Cartesian logic and universal growth, rather

as subtle gestures and impulses for oncoming
meteors, cooling stars extra solar activity.

2

Knee and crag stresses jerk sounds from howling dog
to starling call, yapping percussion and trumpet.

The pheasant possesses the ground upon which it runs
as the altocumulous inhabits the mackerel beds.

Seeking a word to make change I choose voice
the alterotica of accent and localised sensation.

Listen those meandering protons touch more than grass
scattering at mid-latitudes in geomagnetic storms.

My lover's brassy voice looks within and looks around
my body to find arteries, nerves and receptive pores.

She perforates my restless aura regardless of time
absolutely makes me tongue tied at dinner parties.

3

Here in this factory with so many men,
stealing moments, a bike pump, some oil.

The bells! The market! The drove! It's Monday!
Rooting around my beard to find a chisel.

Cecil keeps his pencil behind his ear.
I must burst the bubble in my spirit level.

If you look twice at me I will give you
one finger. No one takes away my fidelity.

Alert to the tactile, brass on wrist,
yet full of mustn't's, don't's, do, do, do.

Touch me. Touch me without fear.
I will walk towards you if I must.

Bunny

hums Crosby's Wooden Ships solo,
the line of defiled, mild, reconciled,
of Christ whose glory lifts the sky,
of forgiveness to the bureaucrat

that did not know his past or dialect
where must lies and how plastic sticks,
stammers yeh, yeh, yeh, not ow
coz Mama said 'soon's dead'.

Bunny has become a votary of hermetics
caravanning at night in a private wood
with a beebalm garden in his head,
an arrangement of groundsel, charity

to the good. Sez 'ello as if he's Eccles
not Mr. Glum and refuses in verbals
with a stag-like insistence on being
a harebell or two away from heaven.

In sacrilege, wreckage and forage
cadging a fag, lift and meal
turning hand and stick by degrees
forever overlooking his lump,

as sly and lowly as a slow worm
legless and nervy
full of swerve and silhouette
skitter and drop.

As slender as a quart turp
coat cut at sixty one
as tight as at thirty one
costrel arched-tailed to town

converting verticals into horizontals
tenuous lineaments into lips
mood into movement to modify staple
to change that restless mark

of dark matter that hangs
in threads by gutters and fences
locked in a web of dishonour
and disreputable sober conduct.

He was to a man told
to bolt the door
burn the hutches, fences, banisters
and make do, and did.

He was to a man sucked
and spat out as too styptic.
His eviction and medical documents miss
his utterances against Dr. Beeching's axe.

Absent-mindedly used the milk deck to fly
not to be here in creamery, granary or dustcart
but there in milk, grain and detritus
and all in a single dwelling preoccupied.

Harmless and harmed less, he marked
his ground with spit, emitted such lip, teeth
to tongue contortions as if he was more
at one with jays and jackdaws.

His gallows humour took him outside
any legal framework, relations
that could not accommodate
guttural purchase.

He was to a man untested
for variant categories of control
and labelling and stood his turf
when confronted by Hancock's nemesis,

having departed the stage as the lord
of misrule with an erect penis,
intent on surviving without electricity
by bicycle and wood nymph.

The Dance of Life

I still see the farm as it is;
a living potential torn apart.
Fields, mud and wood remain
in place. My words do not.

Plant in salad's poison retch
vegetables tilted blue in eyes,
thighs so taut I couldn't move.
Ravaged a year or three too near.

I do not look back to cuts, drained
energy, but forward to fermentation,
twirling my bits again at front 'n'
swerve of Stur's carnival procession.

Huffed tidal tables, sluiced tonics
popped pills, 'd sooner walk the hills
breathing heavy with aching knees.
Signs and sighs outside phonics.

Babbling sinewy burble, river
ground upon which I utter
these make do sounds that gurgle,
clear as a bell in my nutter.

Bunny in the Field

I
Near utmost thirst
set mouth nearest
hole inward touch

possess waste confess
water's timeless bless
tense on wrist

nose first approach
solitude out tipple
not so mindful

after wiping stack
field clear bales
the wind blows

clear from fingers
a delicate tangle
hessian sack boulders

shoulders round cart
cutting away herd
needled all day

the world open
strip stippling stripling
outstretched hands hesitate

or mute attribute
stipend of breast
under his nose

black eyes lashes
stooping to twist
red top alertness

meet eyes meet
meeting warbler song
sunk on iteration

red and black
such allure that
sweeps and moults

II
Bonfire suckles spits
perilously close to
nestled terrified sap

branches hurdles burnt
eyes blaze yorked
yoked choked hapless

not knowing when
not to speak
what must out

shit you like
puss in piss
your bloody ties

more sheen on
surface membrane blink
coppice margin gone

wed blank hours
till price clams
out pastures pastures

that's why I
plant silver syllable
by the brook

and lean back
against the inlay
waste spillage 'n'all

no paperwork on
the casually shot
no archival memory

on 23rd September
old habits huddle
beneath rosy handshakes

I shall be
Today is Christmas
I am sixty

III
Don't drive I
hike ascend descend
maybe spider mend

grass high to
John Deere's finest
black tooth 'n' claw

don't I consider
that this carries
any confirming complicity

as go hither
consequent vacant bridges
crab apple line

course regenerative signs
re ca-ca-call Floyd's
eel crab turnaround

see Sixties ballast
find myself strange
an inevitable inflection

I am placid
yet some shriek
crawling darkness out

I animal figure
tread expressing differential
environment gene against

losses uninsistent stress
elevate veined membrane
gorse rare wings

careful finger placement
to sloe pick
ferric tincture infuse

walk not far
how weathered design
in sharp sentience

Body Aches

Body aches in this tooth faced stump,
the Stour spills and fills my gut with washed
out suds and softened days of non-labour.

A fair day's work for a fair day's pay
knocked around accordingly and at variance
to material acquisition. What now? Not pain!

Hot an' searching meat punches my face, splat
take that filled with not-light and parson's nose.
Ah, hello vicar. Have some sherry. We're eating

late today and not at all. I, of course, never closed
my eyes until it was too late. Those white—reptiles
attack my wizened—bobbing across the water.

Yes, there used to be boating and cunning men
with daggers and bounty ran the bank in ways
more efficient than modern salesmen. I expect you

doubt my ability to run with illusionary tendency
to make a stab at who I really can become and
to drink young Willy under the table, police car.

Then again, I always smoke cigars in The Swan
and talk to Paul Hart about the Blues and painting
a shed full of broken clocks 'n' heels. 'E liked high heels,

put one in a painting of that old man at Ibberton.
You know, what's is name, storyteller. Course they
didn't like Paul at Bryanston coz 'e were poor sna.

I Got the Black Eye

We scored a furrowed line
up at four to bumble and burn
twelve hour shifts, no overtime,
just heat and pressure to sing.

Rooster became Rooster on the deck
turned his attention to the lab girls
started drawing stags everywhere
to show that he wasn't that nutter.

Mick lost three fingers in the mixer
we dug out blood and bone
and kept on salting and turning.
Give it a touch of Irish, Alfie said.

All those pippins, dolly parton's,
rabbit's feet, toad's legs for scrofula,
and told to raise the worm or watch
a goldfinch teasing thistle on waste.

      *   *   *

Cecil and Alfie along the riverbank
rubbing their hands, a counterpoint
to the hollow quills, gutted secondary
annulments that never wash and hard

on their heels, by the gate, wooden leg
woman with a question, red lipstick,
navigating between water filled hoof
marks, broken grass and cow dung.

Can't Can't Say

can't can't say can't can't say can't can't say
ohh ohh ohh ohh ohh ohh   ohh ohh ohh
ohh ohhh ohh ohh ohhh ohh ohh ohhh ohh
can't can't say can't say can't say can't say

tr tr tr tr tr tr tr tr tr tr tr tr tr tr tr
tr   tr   tr   tr   tr
still got plenty o' words in head
in my head tt tt *try try trying*

Yes *my only word* Yes
when I should say No
tr tr tr
ht ht ht ht ht ht ht ht ht

In this becoming bodily sounds affirm
tttt tits words don't keep directions
as much as lip teeth pressure
dispersed with call and flap of wings

m m m em em em erm erm erm
mm mm mm em em em mm mm mm
mem mem mem mem mem mem
Ain't seen Paul. I sez he's dead. Dead.

nnn nnn nnn nnn nnn nnn Yes
Don't need no mind changing
Don't need no left or right decisions
No static new circuit No new codes

can't can't say can't can't say can't say
ohh ohh ohh ohh ohh ohh ohh ohh ohh
ohh ohhh ohhh ohhh ohhh ohh oh oh
can't say can't say can't say can't say

Quiet

What I want is one foot in front of the light. The delicate
choice of where to catch
that old pike, the old wound beneath its crust of blood,
slipping between lily pads,
clogged artery of logs, branches; hip flask of sin

                                           listen

                                     an

                               oak

                         squeaks

                        under

                        air

                  ground

                pressure

                 and

              almost

            topples

into the rush, a drunk

back-racked as often as glisten.

Waders leave before scattered drop.

Stop, stopped loose, moist and well-oxygenated.

Red Dead Nettle
(Badman's posies, Dumb-nettle)

Some tinge like a ponytail
stung my lip, slipped

rattled and smarted word clumps
that spored and blew off course.

Once a noisy grubber
now a Buster Keaton.

In this deficiency muteness unnerves, it is suggestible:
verging on emergency prostrate, it is also to be

as in go to and dig deep
as in membrane barrier from interference

as in photograph the derelicts
isolate damage, erosions and drag.

Burr of goose grass that primes these witnesses,
trims the mane where swirls sinuate.

A Severed Head

Wood vetch, yellow archangel,
grizzled skippers in search of bramble,
scattering of flies, coursing breeze-up.

To the left corner a no-nonsense broiler
solid, no windows, minimal ventilation,
stifling heat, intense spatial allocation.

Some celandine, campion beside a fallen
branch, near the rutted track and fresh
scratchings, revving skid marks.

A severed head

yet no body to be seen
some fizz and filter,

cardinal and stag
not a bluebell in sight

A severed head.

A severed head.

The owner is said to speak pure pidgin.
His entrails must stink.

Yet the activists are as much hunters
as keepers. This step and clearing has no
shame for the voyeur to glean.

Crab apple denoting age, boundary,
deserted apart from a wild service.

A severed head.

Arrowhead

I will my snake belt today

its interlocking boar buckle

as a gesture before Domesday

until the cows leave the parlour

the last thinning of birdsong.

I hold this against the man

who wanted to put his hands

around my neck by the gravel fields.

I hold this against speedcore

the numbed silence of arrest.

I hold this to sun's constancy

the wet field spread pelt

where consciousness is a path

away from intrusions, charges

bandaged hands.

I pick at a buried politics ·

on the edge of belonging

white knuckle scrag

in darkness that smothers

with its ruptures and smears.

You know the yew is transparent

and the raven problem solves

waiting for pliable alphabets

in emergent gullies,

and birthing pools,

where a damselfly

away from the golf course

needs one good eye

as distance rims the vanishing,

one good eye.

This Giddy Bevel

Shrew's nest left of terminus
three feet south south-west
and two feet left of outer ring
by footpath, other rodent prints,
next to barbed wire fence.

Prostrate found sixth spider
among assorted debris, thorns
decomposed clippings. Flints,
axe heads, juniper berries,
bottle, large worn pebbles.

Signs of fox or badger digging
disturbed remains of capsule
medium and small flints three
to nine inches below Oxford
clay, sandstone stresses.

Four inch skull ten inches below.
Assorted small animal bones
within disturbed remains,
twill, gut, indeterminate
deposits, cloying soil texture.

By boundary ditch, second pit
dug in sixteenth century dated
by bottle, cock pheasant. Pale
ash. Gulls above. Tangible
niche of foe and alloy.

Upright, my back aches.
Oft mentioned animals

impinge, smudge, mix
lure, stir in this shaft,
in this giddy bevel.

The Creeper Has Been Out All Night

Creep through fetters, garbled pheasant,
chalked husks of encounter, squeaking
amiss and rent, oh rose thou art sick,
phlebitis to pulmonary embolism.

This way carries the weight of conflict,
Druidic mistletoe, absent finches,
verderers, landowners, keepers,
in defiance, annulment, encroachment.

Chase law, ancient rights expunged,
now Madonna has added fancy trees
to her killing bowl and flown off.
Seek toothwort, valerian, hazel nuts.

Off the track debris, knife edge tension
stoked into fury, tightening snare, snake
in the grass, daubed, veined in black,
pulse race with woodpecker, slate eyes.

The creeper has been out all night.
Dearest I send this to you as a gift.
I have no other beyond my questions.
Keep your song as sharp as a blade.

Signalled As Ox-tongue

As prickly as cow's tongue, borage,
Apollinaire, a pollinating bee bread,
hairy barrach, to allocate courage.

To move from matted hair loss,
unkempt beard to stiff silent thistle type,
chosen to ingratiate, augment, isolate.

I haven't spoken to anyone for days.
I stand rooted with hands that sting and are
sore from the translation of officialdom.

I want to establish the volume of a volume.
I want to write and speak an entirely
different and opportunistic language.

The language of the bristling Ox-tongue
that knows no bounds by the roadside
or in your grandmother's garden.

Scattered Tongue

Scattered tongue is yours to eat

        scraping

tarnish

please,

lay hands on all

laud and curb me once, twice.

You are not my bees

from end to end you are not my Sunday.

To collect, walk those subtle rooms

out of here.

To sin,

        keep on going.

Rank

Rank by ditches in woodland,
creeping shoots, close ranked,
surmounted by racemes of rosy.

T t t tapping. T t t tapping.

Everywhere they are shooting pheasants.
Guns, guns, guns, guns everywhere.
I want to be elsewhere, elsewhere.

Alright there, young'r.
Can't hear much.
Don't know much when you are a weed.

T t t tapping. T t t tapping.

Dad and the lads used to pick conkers for pennies.
Used to pickle them. pick rose hips for syrup.
No one hedges their bets or bifurcates.

Alright there, young'r.
Can hear Cecil and Cyril downstream.
Codlins and cream, small, square, marsh.

T t t tapping. T t t tapping.

Mutterings whispers sniggers.
Above the willow herb,
above the coltsfoot.

T t t tapping. T t t tapping.

When the Redstart Arrives
for jk

When the redstart arrives
I say goodbye to the heron
by the fork and start to shiver
as if the flu were a time slip
rather than a recognition
as if I could drink less
and still possess this slimming
design on my nerves and rise
to put away those pails of
spilt milk that course like lurchers
with their tails between their legs
betwixt and between keepers 'n' finders
and still have time to take back
the bacon or re-consider the fate of those
unaware it is night. And it is night
when there are no lights to put out
nor feral edging only this plump bird
that has come to tap, tap and bob.
I look at this start under candlelight
and swear it has a luminous beak,
black seedy eyes and curse it will
drink me under the table or be turned
into a pirate. I throw corn at this migrant
and consider flight. Oh, no, no. Come back.
I've got more. Look no absolutes, conkers,
insecticides, our mutual track, voracity.
Would sooner chisel and turn my hand,
gouge, every twist tenuous, and avoid the ice.

The Smallest Movement

The smallest movement
that is not the wind
turns my nerves
so that I begin to see

and move carefully

A foot step agitates
my consciousness as
the connecting threads
of a comma

sustain my longevity

from A History of Walking

What has location can be approached
walking across fields marking each loci
with attributes, speech parts, things
to be recalled as and when.

How full the trees, gates, barbed wire
with books and mnemonics,
how cool to store an entire library,
remember the *Divine Comedy*'s maps.

For the Left it is less exercise
more alchemical exploration
a lean on the shoe to the silver seller
a move to everything as something.

To the Right it is an act
in avoidance, display, an indignity
a rush or wander to flit
gestural presences that might.

Bunny's modelled legs are more Chaplinesque
than Wordsworthian knowing that bipedalism
is linked to early laughter and freed
hands lead to intricate manipulation.

This dexterity, anthropologically, knots
with sexual workers, innuendo, hypotheses,
female ancestral hominid predators
and plausible male insecurities. Fantastic!

Stepping Out

I like to keep a simple rhythm
one foot in front of the other
encountering momentum of hoof
and wing and wild lure.

Tangled matter diverges.
One way brings more darkness
in fractured light.
Another and the light stretches, pours.

What was knotted may unravel.
The sequence of identification may
obliterate that sunken deflation
into pure immaculate brilliance.

It is worth living to die in this
conflagration of desire and ideation.
It is the patter of rain upon petal
myriad formations, organisms underfoot.

The realisation that this human value
in loci constitutes and extends
with minimal constant relations
our field of vision.

By Durweston Footbridge

Slowly the landscape reveals itself
as a qubit alive with entanglement.
Each quirk of deposit is a scar
or affectation upon a series of eyelids.

Stones heavy with sleep, rich in tension,
hold scattered gestures, economics
cross-braced with knowledge for this
calming rectitude forced by water.

Each day under the old railway bridge
to this rutted mix of metal displacement
cross-struts of seeing and believing
cling to the sluiced body of botanical feasts.

Tiny islands afford resting places for a heron
and in the foreground, for six years now,
a nest for swans that catch attention
whenever there is pause to scent possibility.

On Focus

I have been looking at the flood plane,
the loss of path, bank and margin,
wondering where the swans retreat,
seeing the landscape without glare
as a string of posts and diluted scum
bubbles marking the central current
with fluttering gulls and wires that sag
in combination with a metallic water,
and keep returning to an obsession
with reinforcing the brook's bank,
removing debris, seeing if I can restore
the stone steps, count the otters downstream
and gauge the fish population.

I am that other with channels and flow,
placement and eye line out of water,
since emptying churns on the deck
circulating with doorstep and cheese block,
the heart cusp open with portly slobber
my gout glass broken into agitation.
I am with the scarcely visible,
the moist acorn waiting to germinate,
the secretly communicative blue grit,
the no-telling habitat, the silt of listening,
the whoops and cries of tawny owls,
waiting heaps of gravel and leaves,
skip and tip hunters, first and second hands,
meandering shadows the size of shires.

Alehoof

Diffused light upon threads of mud,

dead leaves, grass and sandstone

bends to an ache of tight ivy

woven around a withered ash

that seems to call out a bespoke

and dying attachment until the eye

clutches sloes in a muddle of climbing

vegetation and linger of lost worlds

before the arched Victorian brickwork

opens on to a coursing water mill.

Raw Bend: a ripping yarn
for Tom Lowenstein

Drained reeds wrap around and flatter
fences, stumps and grass bank.
There are no gulls, just a light breeze.

Inkpen's Hole, where men and cows fall,
belies its torn and torrid cargo
with blackthorn surface and eddy.

Drying mud clawed and scoured,
seeding thistles, weathered ox-eyes,
beneath tender moss and clover

and those that might simply happen
by and dip aimlessly into
this succulent drinking pool.

Devil's Coach Horse

Kept a devil's coach horse and mealworms as feeder food to observe them turning into beetles. Devil's coach horse started to attack the newly hatched beetles—and this is the strangest thing—never killed any of them, at least not straight off. 6 mealworms turned into beetles and the devil's coach horse pincered them all in the same place between the hind legs and through the left hand wing casing, splitting it in half, all 6 the same. It left them all still very much alive and roaming around the tank, finishing them off after a few days. Devil's coach horse died not knowing when to let go. I found it drowned in a 5mm water saucer with its pincers locked into a mealworm. Its jaws were so stuck I couldn't release them with two toothpicks.

Botanologia
after Gavin Selerie

Adder's Tongue, Alehoof, Love Apples, Mad Apples, Thorny
Apples, Red Archangel, Mild or Spotted Arsmart, Hot or
Biting Arsmart, Bears Breach, Cammock, Lady-Traces,
Clown's Allheal, Creeping Dog's Bane, Earth-Nut, Woody
Eye-Bright, Friars Cowle, Hog's Fennel, Fuss-Balls or Puck
Fists, Crows Garlick, Lady's Bedstraw, Hairy Summer
Chafer, Meme Chanter, Mother of Wine, Pinhole Borer,
Rocket, Succory, Tormentilla, Victorious Viper, Wall Rue,
Yarrow.

Nipplewort

This erect annual found in open woods, hedgerows, waste-
land and rough ground has medicinal and therapeutic
qualities and was once a salad plant. It is much less bitter and
more hairy than dandelion. Used to heal ulcers on women's
nipples, it is also known as Carpenter's Apron, Mary Alone
and Hasty Sergeant. Self-pollinating, it germinates in
autumn and spring and its yellow flowers are visited by bees
in cultivated fields and field margins. The seed is thus in most
cereals. Spreading along the bank it conserves moisture and
prevents erosion. It is less bland than held.

Birch Polypore

Sinking into wet mud along the rutted uphill path with
the constant patter of raindrops on a dense flora of shrubs,
ferns, creepers and moss; I have never felt more alive. Effort
is rewarded by the presence of other living things and the
remnants of rotational coppicing and crabapples. There is an
otherworldly nature to the variation and nature of sounds
and the prospect of encountering stag, tramp or dormice.
Note the dog rose and violet flower of the devil's bit scabious
and its location so that the prospect of the silver washed
fritillary and assorted moths comes ever closer. There are
no old trees. It is mostly hazel, less oak and ash than in the
past, and some pine. It is the smouldering conk that can
be crumbled and made into a restorative tea that I seek. It
appears as the last puff of a dying birch and yet can help save
lives with its antibiotic and anti-inflammatory qualities. Its
rotting wood vaguely smells of apples, It is something that
might be honeyed and sparingly fried with morels, saddle
caps, garlic and eggs as it is full of nourishing vitamins,
heteroglucans and acids but in fact is as tough as old boots.
I can't find any birch and seem to be lost. I am not much of
a wild man really and turn back. I find what could be goat's
beard and see plenty of moths that I am unable to identify.
When I find fallen wood with polypores they are covered
with unappetising moss. Anti-parasites are generous in their
capacities. Upending the wood hidden selves scatter in all
directions.

Broad Oak

A spotted woodpecker drizzles along Broad Oak
feathers in tatters and so bereft of bounce
that I curse such ignorance and strike quickly.

One two three ox eye daisies hit my eyes
yellow flashes bouncing off
and more than spots irritate my mind's eye.

As faded as any relic, the past Broad Oak
seeps through with its King George V,
Autumn Pearmain and pile of leaves.

An owl to the north from Piddles Wood
chats to the walker with its talons,
night vision and escapades, taking a pulse.

In the Thick of It

Prongs of foliage form the head
that supports the gate that swings into action
and rocks the Ham of
the house that Jack built.

Rimmed by a verandah of the heat.

Each leaf signifies hope
welcomes the unknown

apportioned
as wood to breath
these amplify
in the thick of it.

This is a split-level operation
furnace, cutter, skill,
bereft
next to the glow worm trail
and not a sapling, nymph in sight.

Listen.
You can hear the scowls.

Wild Swans at Stur Mill

Faint churr and thrust through rush and lily
until the sluice gates temper and probe.
The water seems to stagnate and browse,
yet lower down it teems, willy nilly.

As the swans test the bank and unknown
the world revolves around them. They could take
flight or pursue other options. They ceremoniously
tread the path to the left. Water glistens, breathing.

Great soap bubbles and froth swirl. Lover after lover,
firm upon stamen and root, tight at nerve ends, edge
stubble and eroded mud to where the river softens
around islands and begins to ripple towards a charge.

Alert and undiminished perception feeds need.
A simple instinct held and executed with all its
attendant dangers from human disturbance, iodine,
hooks, nitrogen overload as the Stur current speeds.

Quietly Turn the Page

Sporadic runs wrap themselves around my head
tsee tsee comes the call as I leave this camouflage
tail propped and flush over bark and new ways.

Waves of martins dive into the ground
and great shoals rear up. So darkly the stain
upsets relations and rearranges the reason.

Regenerative Exchange tips the bolt, rising in its effect
bringing more light, on dankest days, sculptures,
and honour through trust, outside market forces.

We're older now, your breasts pendulous
my arms unfolded, yet we smile at this turn.
A waver of attention as Poles drift.

This feels good. Memories of estrangement,
tussles with the Council, fade outside Yasar's
showing the purpose we really cut,

no longer having mislaid a life.
No, here and aware. Such shading
of the colour may my children never touch.

Be Still and Know That I Was

Be still and know that I was.
Be still and know that in my becoming
wings were beat and veins stressed
that I spoke out and linked arms.

I saw the signature of herbs
within conflicting whorls of possibility.
I saw the roots the voluntary way
reclaiming against the insurmountable.

As if there were no point in not
shifting the word and kicking the tins.
Any lonely place
can suddenly be at the heart of things.

Song Thrush

The song thrush atop the buddleia in full measure
regenerative, translating in such hot, modulated
mimicry and talk that one by one we walk
outside to witness this celebrant, this emissary.

Our minds go back decades to when we last heard
this bird so loud and clear, to see the orchards
and hedgerows when such song burned and coloured
and fruit rolled on the tongue without complaint.

Our wild back garden despised, sniggered at,
and thus anointed by sound and edges of light
in the broader frame of modernity makes us
melt in physical delight and burst out.